Functional Skills
English
Edexcel - Level 1

This nifty little CGP book is full of brilliant practice for Level 1 English. Questions are split into 10-minute tests to help build confidence and provide plenty of useful prep for the Edexcel exam.

We've covered all the key skills needed for the Reading and Writing parts of the test, as well as plenty of spelling, punctuation and grammar practice. There's also a full set of answers at the back — and we've included a handy progress chart to keep track of how students are doing. Nice!

CGP — still the best! ☺

Our sole aim here at CGP is to produce the highest quality books — carefully written, immaculately presented and dangerously close to being funny.

Then we work our socks off to get them out to you — at the cheapest possible prices.

Contents

Part 1 — Reading

Section One — How Texts Present Ideas

Section Two — Reading for Detail

Part 2 — Writing

Section One — Grammar

Section Two — Punctuation

Section Three — Spelling

Section Four — Grammar, Punctuation & Spelling

Section Five — Structure & Format

Published by CGP
Editors: Emma Crighton, Emma Duffee

With thanks to James Summersgill for the proofreading.

With thanks to Alice Dent for the copyright research.

All names, places and incidents are fictitious; any resemblance to actual events or persons is entirely coincidental.

ISBN: 978 1 78908 931 8

Printed by Elanders Ltd, Newcastle upon Tyne.

Clipart from Corel®

How Texts Present Ideas: Test 1

There are **6 questions** in this test.
Give yourself **10 minutes** to answer them all.
You **may** use a dictionary for this test.

Read the leaflet below, then answer the questions.

> Thank you for buying this tree. All you need to do is plant it — here's how:
> 1. Dig a hole in your garden.
> 2. Remove the tree from its container. Be careful not to touch the roots. Do not try to lift the tree up by its leaves (this could kill the tree).
> 3. Put the tree in the hole. Fill any gaps around the base of the tree with soil.
> 4. Water the tree immediately.

If you make a mistake, put a line through the box ☒ and mark your new answer with a cross ☒.

1 What is the **main** purpose of the text?
Put a **cross** ☒ in the correct box.

☐ **A** To describe what trees are like

☐ **B** To persuade people to buy trees

☐ **C** To instruct people how to plant trees

☐ **D** To explain why trees are important

(1

2 Identify **two** things you should not do when removing the tree from the container.

1 .... (1

2 .... (1

3 Name the organisational feature that makes the text easier to follow.

.... (1

Read the advert below, then answer the questions.

> **DO YOU WANT TO PASS YOUR DRIVING TEST FIRST TIME?**
> **DO YOU WANT A FRIENDLY, EXPERIENCED INSTRUCTOR?**
>
> If your answer to both of these questions is **yes**, call me on 07700 900472 and **book** your first driving lesson **today**!
>
> I am a qualified driving instructor with over 10 years of experience. I have helped over 100 people pass their test, with many of them passing first time. Whether you've never driven or you're struggling to pass your test, I can help you to become confident behind the wheel.
>
> Sign up for nine lessons and get your tenth lesson **FREE**.
>
> FOR THE BEST IN THE BUSINESS, CALL ***DINA'S DRIVING***!

4 **According to the text, how many people has Dina helped to pass their driving test?**

.... (1)

5 **Read the phrase below and circle to say whether it is a fact or an opinion.**

'the best in the business' **Fact / Opinion** (1)

6 **Which two of these language features are used in the text to persuade readers to call Dina? Put a cross ☒ in the correct boxes.**

If you make a mistake, put a line through the box ☒ and mark your new answer with a cross ☒.

☐ **A** Rhetorical question

☐ **B** Caption

☐ **C** Rule of three

☐ **D** Command

(2)

END OF TEST **/ 8**

How Texts Present Ideas: Test 2

There are **4 questions** in this test.
Give yourself **10 minutes** to answer them all.
You **may** use a dictionary for this test.

Read the reviews below, then answer the questions.

Reviews of Hydra Mobile 2E

1,625 Reviews

WRITE A REVIEW

Brilliant Phone

Michelle Peabody

After my last mobile phone stopped working, I bought myself a Hydra 2E and it is probably the best decision I have ever made. This phone is cheap, elegant and easy to use. It has all the features you need in a good mobile, such as a great camera and lots of storage for apps and music.

Some people say it is inconvenient because it is too big — admittedly, it doesn't fit in my pocket and is difficult to carry around without a bag. However, I like having a big screen for watching videos, so I don't really mind. My only criticism is that the battery runs out of charge pretty quickly.

Everybody should buy this phone!

Okay, but not great

Rohit Agarwal

I was really excited to get this mobile, but I have been a bit disappointed with it so far. I am happy about the price because it was cheap, but it has lots of problems. It is quite difficult to use because it is too big to hold in my hand and I can't fit it in my pocket — this really annoys me. I have also found that the camera is worse than my old phone — all my photos look a bit blurry. I wouldn't advise people to buy this phone. It works, but you can buy a much better phone for only a little more money.

1 Name the organisational feature that Michelle used to structure her review.

.... (1

2 Which **two** of these language features are used in the first review to show the Hydra 2E is a good phone?
Put a **cross** ☒ in the correct boxes.

If you make a mistake, put a line through the box ☒ and mark your new answer with a cross ☒.

☐ **A** Slogan

☐ **B** Alliteration

☐ **C** Rule of three

☐ **D** Exclamation

(2)

---

3 The text includes facts and opinions. Which **two** of the following statements are facts? Put a **cross** ☒ in the correct boxes.

☐ **A** 'it is inconvenient because it is too big'

☐ **B** The Hydra 2E has over 1000 reviews.

☐ **C** 'I bought myself a Hydra 2E'

☐ **D** 'I like having a big screen for watching videos'

(2)

---

4 **(a)** Identify **one** opinion that is the same in Review 1 and Review 2.

....

.... (1)

(b) Give **one** quotation from both Review 1 and Review 2 to support your answer.

Review 1 ....

.... (1)

Review 2 ....

.... (1)

END OF TEST

/8

How Texts Present Ideas: Test 3

There are **5 questions** in this test.
Give yourself **10 minutes** to answer them all.
You **may** use a dictionary for this test.

Read the informational leaflet below, then answer the questions.

HILTGATE FOOD BANK

Food Poverty Crisis in the UK

Not being able to afford enough food to have a healthy diet is known as food poverty. In the UK, up to 3 million people are undernourished and about 4 million children are living in poverty. 1 in 6 parents say they have missed meals to feed their children.

What is a food bank?

A food bank stocks food and basic supplies to give to people who need them, free of charge. There are 2000 food banks across the UK.

Hiltgate Food Bank provides free food to people in Hiltgate and the surrounding area. On weekends, they also provide hot food.

What can you do to support us?

1. Donate food

Hiltgate Food Bank desperately needs food donations in order to feed people in need. Donating food is easy — simply drop it off at Hiltgate's school, church or supermarket. We would be especially grateful to receive canned vegetables, pasta and rice.

2. Volunteer with us

We need volunteers to help with sorting and packaging all of the donations. If you are interested in volunteering, please email us at: hiltgatefoodbank@azmail.co.uk.

Please help us fight food poverty in Hiltgate. Donate and volunteer now.

1 What does the photo suggest volunteers do at Hiltgate food bank?

....

.... (1

2 Circle the option that best describes the tone of each of the phrases below.

(a) 'There are 2000 food banks' **Personal / Impersonal** (1)

(b) 'We need volunteers' **Personal / Impersonal** (1)

---

3 **(a)** What is the subheading of the section that tells you how to help food banks?

.... (1)

(b) What is the subheading of the section that introduces Hiltgate Food Bank?

.... (1)

---

4 The text includes facts and opinions. Which **two** of the following statements are opinions? Put a **cross** ☒ in the correct boxes.

If you make a mistake, put a line through the box ☒ and mark your new answer with a cross ☒.

☐ **A** It's easy to donate food to the food bank.

☐ **B** It's better to donate food than volunteer.

☐ **C** Food banks stock food and basic supplies.

☐ **D** You don't have to pay at food banks. (2)

---

5 What is the **main** purpose of this text? Put a **cross** ☒ in the correct box.

☐ **A** To argue food banks are important

☐ **B** To instruct people to use food banks

☐ **C** To persuade people to donate or volunteer

☐ **D** To explain how to cook hot food (1)

END OF TEST **/ 8**

How Texts Present Ideas: Test 4

There are **6 questions** in this test.
Give yourself **10 minutes** to answer them all.
You **may** use a dictionary for this test.

Read the webpage below, then answer the questions.

MENU

Most Read Articles

1. Benod: Top 5 Places to Eat
2. Midweek Dinner Ideas
3. Recipe Time: Cupcakes

About the Author

Jade Elliott is a writer and restaurant critic. She started her career by writing recipes for a student magazine, before joining our site in 2017.

Tea-riffic: My Favourite Café

If there's one thing I love more than a nice cup of tea, it's a great café to drink it in. A café is about more than just the drinks it serves; it needs to be a unique place where customers can retreat with a book or socialise with friends.

That's why my favourite café is 'Tea-riffic'. Not only does it make excellent cups of tea, but it truly feels like a second home. When you walk in, you are immediately greeted by the welcoming smell of coffee and freshly-baked biscuits. The walls are lined with bookcases and signs that advertise 'Gorgeously Gooey Brownies' — a slogan I can never resist.

1 Which **one** of these language features is used in the text to persuade readers?
Put a **cross** ☒ in the correct box.

If you make a mistake, put a line through the box ☒ and mark your new answer with a cross ☒.

☐ **A** Metaphor

☐ **B** Alliteration

(1

2 How did the author of the article on the webpage start their career?

....

(1

3 Is this text descriptive or instructive?
Give **one** example from the text to support your answer.

....

....

(2

Read the letter below, then answer the questions.

> **Grizton Council**
> Educate, Innovate, Excel
>
> Dear Resident,
>
> We are writing to inform you about changes to public transport in Grizton.
>
> **What's changing?**
> As you may know, Grizton railway station is in need of major repairs after severe flood damage last winter. In light of this, repair work on the station is scheduled to begin in January and will last for approximately 12 months.
>
> There will be reduced train services during this period. However, a temporary bus service will be available to make sure everyone can still get out and about.
>
> If you have any questions about these changes, please visit the Grizton Council website.

4 Which **two** of the quotations below are examples of informal language? Put a **cross** ☒ in the correct boxes.

If you make a mistake, put a line through the box ☒ and mark your new answer with a cross ☒.

☐ **A** 'We are writing to inform you'

☐ **B** 'What's changing?'

☐ **C** 'everyone can still get out and about'

☐ **D** 'please visit the Grizton Council website.'

(2)

5 Write down the slogan used by Grizton Council.

.... (1)

6 According to the text, why does Grizton railway station need major repairs?

.... (1)

END OF TEST /8

How Texts Present Ideas: Test 5

There are **5 questions** in this test.
Give yourself **10 minutes** to answer them all.
You **may** use a dictionary for this test.

Read the articles below, then answer the questions.

Article A

Work Experience Is Essential

To get a job, most employers want you to have relevant experience, so getting some work experience is vital. Not only does it look good on your CV, but it can give you a feel for what the actual job would be like. Work experience also lets you develop skills which are useful for the role. However, the most important reason to do work experience is to confirm whether you are actually interested in the job. If you don't enjoy your time doing work experience, you should think about looking for a different job!

How to make the most of work experience:

- Show enthusiasm.
- Be willing to get stuck in — work experience is a great opportunity to try new things and learn new skills.
- Don't be afraid to ask questions.

Article B

Focus On Other Avenues

Work experience can be really useful, but only if you choose the right company. I found some of my work experience fairly poor because I was doing jobs I had no interest in. I want to be a receptionist but I worked in a garage and as a gardener. Even when I did manage to get work experience as a receptionist, I didn't learn many skills that are useful for the job — I spent most of the time making coffee. However, being able to talk to the current receptionists helped to confirm that it is the job I want to do. It also allowed me to develop a connection with a potential future employer, which was really useful.

How to make the most of work experience:

- Ask lots of questions.
- Make sure it is relevant to the job that you are interested in.

1 Identify **two** organisational features that are used in both of the articles.

1 .... (1)

2 .... (1)

2 Give **one** opinion about work experience from Article B.

.... (1)

3 Which quotation below is an example of language that instructs the reader? Put a **cross** ☒ in the correct box.

If you make a mistake, put a line through the box ☒ and mark your new answer with a cross ☒.

☐ **A** 'Not only does it look good on your CV'

☐ **B** 'I worked in a garage and as a gardener.'

☐ **C** 'Work experience can be really useful'

☐ **D** 'Show enthusiasm.'

(1)

---

4 Give **one** opinion that is the same in the two articles.

....

.... (1)

---

5 **(a)** Give **one** opinion that is different in Article A and Article B.

....

.... (1)

(b) Give **one** example from **both** Article A and Article B to support your answer to part (a).

Article A ....

.... (1)

Article B ....

.... (1)

END OF TEST / 8

How Texts Present Ideas: Test 6

There are **5 questions** in this test.
Give yourself **10 minutes** to answer them all.
You **may** use a dictionary for this test.

Read the webpage below, then answer the questions.

North Sea Hockey Club

Search

Home | **About Us** | **News** | **Photos** | **Membership** | **Contact Us!**

Welcome to North Sea Hockey Club!

We are a growing local club with over 50 members. We have two men's and two women's teams, ranging from beginner to advanced hockey.

Whether you've never picked up a hockey stick or you're an experienced player, we guarantee that North Sea Hockey Club is the club for you!

Men's District League

Club	Points	Position
Ulverbury	11	1
North Sea	8	2
Upthwaite	7	3
South Lake	3	4

We train twice a week — on Mondays and Fridays at 7 pm. It's up to you whether you join for both sessions or just one. Matches take place on Saturday or Sunday afternoons. We have monthly socials where the whole club gets together for a drink.

What our members say:

'I first learnt how to play hockey at North Sea when I was seven and have been playing for the club ever since. It's a really sociable club and I've made so many amazing friends here.'

Edith, 24

'I love playing for North Sea because we have a good coach and we're doing really well in the league.'

Tamal, 32

1 Identify a quotation that tells you when North Sea's hockey matches take place.

.... (1)

2 Name the webpage feature you would use to:

(a) Get in touch with North Sea Hockey Club .... (1)

(b) Search the website for more information .... (1)

---

3 The text includes facts and opinions.
Which **two** of the following statements are facts?
Put a **cross** ☒ in the correct boxes.

If you make a mistake, put a line through the box ☒ and mark your new answer with a cross ☒.

☐ **A** North Sea Hockey Club has four teams in total.

☐ **B** Members should go to both training sessions.

☐ **C** There is a social event every month.

☐ **D** North Sea Hockey Club has a really good coach. (2)

---

4 Which **one** of these language features is used in the text to persuade readers to join North Sea Hockey Club?
Put a **cross** ☒ in the correct box.

☐ **A** Abbreviation

☐ **B** Direct address

☐ **C** Idiom

☐ **D** Simile (1)

---

5 **(a)** According to the text, who is currently first in the men's hockey league?

.... (1)

(b) Identify **one** feature that helped you find this information.

.... (1)

END OF TEST | **/ 8**

How Texts Present Ideas: Test 7

There are **6 questions** in this test.
Give yourself **10 minutes** to answer them all.
You **may** use a dictionary for this test.

Read the interview below, then answer the questions.

Jack Dobbs has been a party planner at 'Perfect Party Plans' for six years. He met up with us to talk about what it's like to work in the party business.

Interviewer: "What's your favourite thing about being a party planner?"

Jack: "I love my job, so it's difficult to just choose one aspect of it! Two of my favourite things are inventing new ideas for parties and seeing my customers enjoy the parties I've organised. Watching them laughing, dancing and spending time with their friends and family — that's what makes it all worth it."

Interviewer: "Are there any bad bits then?"

Jack: "Well, it's not all laughter and cake. As you can imagine, party planning is stressful because everything needs to be ready by a specific date, which is easier said than done. That said, when it all comes together, it's amazing."

1 Identify **one positive** thing and **one negative** thing Jack says about being a party planner.

Positive .... (1)

Negative .... (1)

---

2 Which quotation from the text below is an example of informal language?
Put a **cross** ☒ in the correct box.

If you make a mistake, put a line through the box ☒ and mark your new answer with a cross ☒.

☐ **A** 'Well, it's not all laughter and cake'

☐ **B** 'party planning is stressful'

☐ **C** 'everything needs to be ready by a specific date'

☐ **D** 'difficult to just choose one aspect'

(1)

Read the advert below, then answer the questions.

ZOO PARTY

When? Saturday 28th November, 2 PM
Price: £1 per person*

Bring your children down to Ludtow Community Hall for an incredible zoo-themed party, thrown by the local youth group! There will be face-painting, pass-the-parcel, jungle music and much more. Parents can enjoy a soft drink and a piece of homemade cake whilst supervising their children.
Children under the age of eight must be supervised at all times.

*Children under four go free!

3 **According to the text, who has organised the party?**

.... (1)

4 **You may use a dictionary to answer this question.**

'Children under the age of eight must be supervised at all times.'

Suggest one word or phrase that could replace 'supervised' without changing the meaning of the quotation.

.... (1)

5 **Identify one thing adults can enjoy at the event.**

.... (1)

6 **(a)** **According to the text, who can go to the party for free?**

.... (1)

(b) **Identify one feature that helped you find this information.**

.... (1)

END OF TEST **/ 8**

How Texts Present Ideas: Test 8

There are **6 questions** in this test.
Give yourself **10 minutes** to answer them all.
You **may** use a dictionary for this test.

Read the magazine article below, then answer the questions.

Escape to the Lakes

Chimamanda Farah

Every week I travel around the UK looking for the best places to visit. This week I explored the Lake District, located in the northwest of England.

1. The Weather

The Lake District, England's largest national park, is well known for its towering mountains, peaceful valleys and, of course, its lakes. But, as my husband reminded me before I set off on the five hour train journey to get there, it's equally famous for its rain. So, having packed my raincoat, my umbrella, several thick pairs of socks and my wellies, off I went. I was very glad to have taken all this waterproof gear — it rained for almost the entire duration of my visit!

2. The Stunning Views

Whether the rain is pouring or mist is descending onto the mountains, the Lake District is surely one of the most beautiful places in the UK. On a friend's suggestion, I climbed one of the mountains overlooking Lake Windermere and was in utter awe of the view. There was water and hillside stretching for as far as the eye could see.

3. Plenty to Do

The Lake District is not only a brilliant place for walking, but for any outdoor activity — from cycling and kayaking, to swimming and running. Once you've tired yourself out with all that exercise, you can settle down in a café or browse the shops in one of the towns which are scattered throughout the hills.

In summary, I would strongly encourage everyone to visit the Lake District, even if it is a bit wet.

1 According to the text, where in England is the Lake District located?

.... (1)

2 Name the lake that made the author experience a feeling of 'utter awe'.

.... (1)

3 According to the text, how did the writer get to the Lake District?

.... (1)

4 Identify **two** organisational features that have been used in the text.

1 .... (1)

2 .... (1)

5 Which of the options below is **not** a purpose of this article?
Put a **cross** ☒ in the correct box.

If you make a mistake, put a line through the box ☒ and mark your new answer with a cross ☒.

☐ **A** To describe the attractions of the Lake District

☐ **B** To persuade the reader to visit the Lake District

☐ **C** To advise the reader about activities in the Lake District

☐ **D** To instruct the reader on how to get to the Lake District (1)

6 Which **two** things does the image in the text tell you about kayaking?
Put a **cross** ☒ in the correct boxes.

☐ **A** It is permitted to kayak in the Lake District.

☐ **B** Kayaking can be a group activity.

☐ **C** Kayaking is a good activity for beginners.

☐ **D** It is cheap to rent kayaks. (2)

END OF TEST

/ 8

Reading for Detail: Test 1

There are **6 questions** in this test.
Give yourself **10 minutes** to answer them all.
You **may** use a dictionary for this test.

Read the webpage below, then answer the questions.

Fuss-free Holidays

Chilled holidays that set you free.

Search

Home	Holidays	**Destinations**	Hotels

DISCOVER MAREAU — AN IDYLLIC FRENCH LAKESIDE RETREAT

Tucked away on the edge of the Alps, Mareau sits at the side of the tranquil Lake Antaux, surrounded by farmland and snow-capped mountains.

Step back in time...

Originally a little fishing town, Mareau is now a popular tourist destination. Wander around the old town and take in the medieval churches, cobbled streets and French cafés. Make sure to visit Mareau Chateau, a sixteenth-century castle which overlooks the town, to learn about Mareau's fascinating past.

Get outdoors...

Lake Antaux is Mareau's most popular attraction, with crystal-clear water and sandy beaches. It's the ideal place for a whole range of activities, from sunbathing to swimming. You can hire bikes and cycle around the lake, or relax on the beach with an ice cream.

Visitor Review...

"Mareau is the most beautiful, tranquil place I have ever visited!" — Amélie, 26

Upcoming Flights: London to Mareau

Date	Price
Fri 6 May	£24
Sat 7 May	£24
Sun 8 May	£28

Click here to **browse budget flights**!

1 **(a)** What is the subheading of the section that tells you about Mareau's history?

.... (1)

(b) What is the subheading of the section that tells you about activities near the lake?

.... (1)

2 Using the text, identify **two** types of building you can see in Mareau.

1 ....

2 .... (2)

3 How much would it cost to fly from London to Mareau on Sunday 8th May?

.... (1)

4 You may use a dictionary to answer this question.

'Discover Mareau — an idyllic French lakeside retreat'

Suggest **one** word or phrase that could replace 'idyllic' without changing the meaning of the quotation.

.... (1)

5 "Mareau is the most beautiful, tranquil place I have ever visited!"
Why are quotation marks used here?
Put a cross ☒ in the correct box.

If you make a mistake, put a line through the box ☒ and mark your new answer with a cross ☒.

☐ **A** To show that the words are speech

☐ **B** To introduce a list

☐ **C** To show Amélie is asking a question

☐ **D** To show the sentence is an exclamation (1)

6 According to the text, what is the most popular tourist attraction in Mareau?

.... (1)

END OF TEST **/ 8**

Reading for Detail: Test 2

There are **5 questions** in this test.
Give yourself **10 minutes** to answer them all.
You **may** use a dictionary for this test.

Read the emails below, then answer the questions.

To: nadiya.burn@azmail.co.uk
Subject: Job Hunting — help!

Dear Nadiya,

I'm currently looking for a job and I would really appreciate your help.

I've been applying for various jobs for a few weeks now but it's really de-motivating. I have been rejected every single time. So many companies don't even send a reply and I always feel left in the dark about my application. I want to concede defeat, but I know I shouldn't.

You've got a job doing something you love, so how did you do it? Do you have any tips on making a successful job application? I think it's best to send out lots of job applications for any job I can find, but what do you think?

Thanks so much for your help,

Matthew

To: matthew.nowak@azmail.co.uk
Subject: RE: Job Hunting — help!

Dear Matthew,

I'm sorry to hear that you're feeling that way. I'd be happy to collaborate with you!

I can relate to your situation — I applied for loads of jobs over several months and was constantly rejected. This was bad for my mental health and I wanted to give up.

However, I did eventually find a company that I loved and that also loved me! I think that's the key to it: don't just apply for loads of jobs. Apply for jobs you have a genuine interest in, because that passion will shine through. You could also try doing some work experience. If a company likes you, they might offer you a full-time job.

Good luck with your applications,

Nadiya

1 **According to the text, how long has Matthew been applying for jobs?**

.... (1)

2 **'You've got a job doing something you love, so how did you do it?'**
Why is the question mark used here?

.... (1)

3 You can use a dictionary for this question.

(a) 'I have been rejected every single time'
Suggest **one** word or phrase that could replace 'rejected' without changing the meaning of the quotation.

.... (1)

(b) 'I'd be happy to collaborate with you!'
Suggest **one** word or phrase that could replace 'collaborate' without changing the meaning of the quotation.

.... (1)

---

4 Identify **one** quotation from the text that shows that Matthew is unhappy.

.... (1)

---

5 **(a)** Give **one** opinion that is different in Matthew's email and Nadiya's email.

....

.... (1)

(b) Give **one** example from **each** email to support your answer to part (a).

Matthew's email ....

.... (1)

Nadiya's email ....

.... (1)

END OF TEST

/8

Reading for Detail: Test 3

There are **4 questions** in this test.
Give yourself **10 minutes** to answer them all.
You **may** use a dictionary for this test.

Read the forum posts below, then answer the questions.

Gluten-Free: have your say

Post a reply | Start a new thread

Gluten-free, fun-free?

Becca Forum Member Posted: 30th November 10:16

My doctor recently diagnosed me with coeliac disease (a digestive condition which means my body reacts badly to gluten). She told me I have to follow a strict gluten-free diet, but I'm finding it really difficult because it turns out there is gluten in all my favourite foods — pasta, bread, cakes, etc.
The gluten-free versions of many foods aren't as nice as "regular" versions and they're also more expensive. It's even tricky to do things like visit restaurants, because now I have to read the menu carefully and there are way less options. I sometimes feel really self-conscious when I have to ask for special food. What are other people's experiences of gluten-free diets?

Reply to 'Gluten-free, fun-free?'

Abdul Forum Member Posted: 30th November 11:34

Hi Becca! I've had coeliac disease for five years. I can definitely sympathise about the price of gluten-free food — it's crazy that a loaf of gluten-free bread costs £3! However, I would say that the range and quality of gluten-free substitutes has really improved in recent years. In fact, my friends (who don't have coeliac disease) often say they can't tell the difference between gluten-free and "regular" food! Restaurants are also better than they used to be — food labelling is now much better and I find that waiters are normally really well-informed about dietary requirements. If you feel self-conscious asking for special options at restaurants, maybe you could try calling ahead to find out what choices they have, or looking at their menu online before you go? Don't worry, it gets easier over time!

1 You can use a dictionary for this question.

'a digestive condition which means my body reacts badly to gluten'

Suggest **one** word or phrase that could replace 'condition' without changing the meaning of the quotation.

.... (1)

---

2 Circle the correct answer to each of the questions below.

(a) Who complains that gluten-free options are limited? **Becca** / **Abdul** (1)

(b) Who has had coeliac disease for longer? **Becca** / **Abdul** (1)

---

3 'it's crazy that a loaf of gluten-free bread costs £3!'
Why is the exclamation mark used here?
Put a **cross** ☒ in the **two** correct boxes.

If you make a mistake, put a line through the box and mark your new answer with a cross ☒.

☐ **A** To show the end of the sentence

☐ **B** To show possession

☐ **C** To show a strong emotion

☐ **D** To provide extra information (2)

---

4 **(a)** Give **one** opinion that is the same in Becca's post and Abdul's post.

.... (1)

(b) Give **one** example from **each** post to support your answer to part (a).

Becca's post ....

.... (1)

Abdul's post ....

.... (1)

END OF TEST **/ 8**

Reading for Detail: Test 4

There are **5 questions** in this test.
Give yourself **10 minutes** to answer them all.
You **may** use a dictionary for this test.

Read the leaflet below, then answer the questions.

HAVE FUN, GET FIT!

When?
7-8 pm every Tuesday

Where?
Delton Sports Centre

Do you want to **get into shape** without spending hours in the gym? Do you want to **enjoy** exercise rather than slogging away on a treadmill?

WE HAVE A **SOLUTION**: SIGN UP TO **FUN FUSION** CLASSES **TODAY**!

Break out of the boredom of your exercise routine with Fun Fusion — we fuse together **multiple forms** of exercise to make you work twice as hard, and with **twice the fun**!

Our classes combine yoga, pilates, weight training and cardio in an epic fusion which improves everything from fitness and endurance to flexibility and mobility.

Every week, our **expert instructors** will put you through your paces with a new workout that's freshly choreographed and **specially tailored** to the interests of the class.

Come along on **Tuesday** to try out Fun Fusion for just **£4**.[1]

[1] After week one, the price rises to £5 per class.

1 Write down whether each statement is true or false.

'Fun Fusion' classes only involve one form of exercise. ....

'Fun Fusion' classes take place on Tuesdays. .... (2)

2 Identify **one** thing that the photograph tells you about 'Fun Fusion' classes.

.... (1)

3 **(a)** According to the text, where do 'Fun Fusion' classes take place?

.... (1)

(b) Identify **one** feature that helped you find this information.

.... (1)

---

4 You may use a dictionary to answer this question.

'specially tailored to the interests of the class'

Suggest **one** word or phrase that could replace 'tailored to' without changing the meaning of the quotation.

.... (1)

---

5 **(a)** What is the main purpose of this leaflet? Put a **cross** ☒ in the correct box.

☐ **A** To explain why exercising is good for you

☐ **B** To persuade people to sign up to 'Fun Fusion'

☐ **C** To instruct people how to exercise

☐ **D** To describe how to do a 'Fun Fusion' workout (1)

If you make a mistake, put a line through the box ☒ and mark your new answer with a cross ☒.

(b) Give **one** example from the text to support your answer to part (a).

.... (1)

END OF TEST **/ 8**

Grammar: Test 1

There are **6 questions** in this test.
Give yourself **10 minutes** to answer them all.
You **may not** use a dictionary for this test.

1 Circle the correct option in each sentence below.

(a) I am looking forward to finding **a / the** new job. (1)

(b) I wanted **a / an** apple, but there was only a banana available. (1)

---

2 'There is three people doing the interview.'

(a) Which word in this sentence is incorrect?

.... (1)

(b) Rewrite the sentence with the mistake corrected.

.... (1)

3

The bus should of been here 10 minutes ago.

Rewrite this sentence using correct grammar.

.... (1)

4 The two sentences below have been split apart and mixed up.

for my budget.	The recipe seems perfect for me
because it looks delicious.	However, it is a bit too expensive

Write the sentences out with all the parts in the correct order.

....

....

.... (2)

---

5 Underline the **verb** in the sentence below.

'I completed my paperwork last week.' (1)

---

6 Use 'although', 'until' and 'after' to complete the sentences below.
You can only use each joining word **once**.

The instructions were clear .... it was still hard to build.

Selena went to visit her friend .... finishing her shift.

I kept waking up late .... I bought a new alarm clock. (2)

END OF TEST

/ 10

Grammar: Test 2

There are **5 questions** in this test.
Give yourself **10 minutes** to answer them all.
You **may not** use a dictionary for this test.

1 Use 'but', 'so' and 'nor' to complete the sentences below.
You can only use each joining word **once**.

Susan wants to get a promotion, ... she has been working harder.

Darren doesn't like running, ... does he like swimming.

She can speak Polish, ... she can't speak French. (2)

---

2 Write out the sentences below in the past tense.

(a) Pavel tries to pay his rent.

.... (1)

(b) They need to find a new job.

.... (1)

(c) Emily runs every morning before work.

.... (1)

3 Circle the correct option in the sentence below.

She **win** / **wins** most of her tennis matches when she focuses properly. (1)

---

4 The sentence below has been split apart and mixed up.

and finally I cleaned the kitchen.	then I took my children to school
pick up my dry cleaning,	I went to

Rewrite the sentence with all the parts in the correct order.

....

....

.... (2)

---

5 Write out the sentences below, using 'will' to make them about the future.

(a) I have seen that film.

.... (1)

(b) Shania was not very impressed.

.... (1)

END OF TEST **/ 10**

Grammar: Test 3

There are **7 questions** in this test.
Give yourself **10 minutes** to answer them all.
You **may not** use a dictionary for this test.

1 Circle the correct option in each sentence below.

(a) They are often woken up when their dog **bark / barks** at night. (1)

(b) My friends **want / wants** to go on holiday together soon. (1)

---

2 For each sentence below, identify the **verb** and the **person** that the action is being done to.

(a) The broken tap sprayed water all over Megan.

Verb .... Person .... (1)

(b) The doctor operated on her patient.

Verb .... Person .... (1)

---

3 Underline the **article** in the sentence below.

'It is getting very cold in the evenings.' (1)

---

4 Use an appropriate verb to complete the sentence below.

Hussein .... his CV last night and was very pleased with it. (1)

---

5 Which of the sentences below talks about the future correctly?
Put a **cross** ☒ in the correct box.

If you make a mistake, put a line through the box ☒ and mark your new answer with a cross ☒.

☐ **A** She will goes to see her new house next week.

☐ **B** I are going to prepare for the week ahead.

☐ **C** I will go to the meeting that has been arranged.

☐ **D** He am going to drive to pick his children up.

(1)

6

I am <u>visited</u> my cousin to see their new house.

Rewrite this sentence, putting the underlined verb in the correct tense.

.... (1)

---

7 'Munira fall off her bike, but she only scraped her knee.'

(a) Why is this sentence incorrect?

.... (1)

(b) Rewrite the sentence with the mistake corrected.

.... (1)

END OF TEST **/ 10**

Punctuation: Test 1

There are **6 questions** in this test.
Give yourself **10 minutes** to answer them all.
You **may not** use a dictionary for this test.

1 Which of the sentences below uses full stops correctly?
Put a **cross** ☒ in the correct box.

If you make a mistake, put a line through the box ☒ and mark your new answer with a cross ☒.

☐ **A** Cumbria is cold. and it's one of the rainiest places in England.

☐ **B** Bolu realised she had forgotten. to send some of the invitations

☐ **C** She was scared because she had never driven at night.

☐ **D** Do you want to have a starter before your main course. (1)

---

2 I need to pack a suit a shirt a toothbrush and a hairbrush.

Rewrite this sentence, adding **two** commas in the correct places.

....

.... (1)

---

3 Circle the correct option in each sentence below.

(a) **Its** / **It's** far too cold to be walking outside without a coat. (1)

(b) My cat has been cleaning **its** / **it's** fur a lot recently. (1)

4 "Oh, that is so generous of you. Youre very kind."

(a) Why is this sentence incorrect?

.... (1)

(b) Write the sentence out with the mistake corrected.

.... (1)

---

5 You are going out for a meal tonight.

Rewrite this sentence as a question.

.... (1)

---

6 Rewrite the sentences below, adding capital letters in the correct places.

(a) there were a lot of cars on the main road to manchester.

.... (1)

(b) antonio needs to send a parcel to his mother in italy.

.... (1)

(c) during her break on monday, jane went for a short walk.

.... (1)

END OF TEST **/ 10**

Punctuation: Test 2

There are **5 questions** in this test.
Give yourself **10 minutes** to answer them all.
You **may not** use a dictionary for this test.

1 Rewrite each sentence below, adding an apostrophe to show ownership.

(a) I prefer quiet villages to Londons busy streets.

.... (1)

(b) All three of Kevins dogs are labradors.

.... (1)

2 The text below is missing three punctuation marks.

I thought the show would be a bit more expensive Are the children's tickets really that cheap That's absolutely amazing value

Rewrite the text above, adding in **one** full stop, **one** exclamation mark and **one** question mark.

....

....

....

.... (3)

3 Please show me how i should fill out this form

Rewrite this sentence, punctuating it correctly.

.... (1)

4 **Add the correct punctuation in the boxes below to complete the passage.**

As Obafemi rushed around the shop ☐ he looked at the list of things that Mary had asked him to buy. He started to panic — the shop was going to close soon. Could he find all of the items in time ☐ (2)

5 'The apartment has a bedroom a kitchen and a bathroom.'

(a) Why is this sentence incorrect?

.... (1)

(b) Rewrite the sentence with the mistake corrected.

....

.... (1)

END OF TEST **/ 10**

Spelling: Test 1

There are **5 questions** in this test.
Give yourself **10 minutes** to answer them all.
You **may not** use a dictionary for this test.

1 Some people didn't get there packages.

Rewrite the sentence above, correcting any spelling mistakes.

.... (1)

2 **Circle the correct option in each sentence below.**

(a) I'm working hard to **achieve / acheive** my dreams. (1)

(b) I am busy this weekend — I have to paint my **cieling / ceiling**. (1)

(c) I have been interested in **science / sceince** since I was a child. (1)

3 **Write the correct spelling of each word below.**

(a) discribe .... (1)

(b) suprise .... (1)

4 Which of the words below is spelt correctly?
Put a **cross** ☒ in the correct box.

☐ **A** arested

☐ **B** commanding

☐ **C** carefull

☐ **D** unnsure

If you make a mistake, put a line through the box ☒ and mark your new answer with a cross ☒.

(1)

---

5 The passage below contains **three** spelling mistakes.

Rosie was dissappointed when her show was cancelled. Her friends saw this and tryed to cheer her up. After spending the rest of the day laughing and jokeing with them, Rosie began to feel better.

Rewrite the passage using the correct spellings.

....

....

....

....

....

.... (3)

END OF TEST

/ 10

Spelling: Test 2

There are **6 questions** in this test.
Give yourself **10 minutes** to answer them all.
You **may not** use a dictionary for this test.

1 The sentence below contains the shortened form of a longer word.

She tried to read the whole book, but gave up after reading the <u>intro</u>.

Write out the longer form of the underlined word.

.... (1)

---

2 He was tired and stressed, which made him unecessarily rude.

Rewrite the sentence above, correcting any spelling mistakes.

....

.... (1)

---

3 Write the plural form of each word below.

(a) deer .... (1)

(b) child .... (1)

(c) lorry .... (1)

4 You shouldn't try to do to many jobs at the same time.

Rewrite the sentence above, correcting any spelling mistakes.

....

.... (1)

5 Circle the correct option in the sentence below.

Chris looked at the **stuning** / **stunning** artwork and was amazed. (1)

6 The passage below contains **three** spelling mistakes.

Declan had just acepted an offer for his antique knifes and felt pleased. He knew that the sale would be good for his bisness.

Rewrite the passage using the correct spellings.

....

....

.... (3)

END OF TEST

/ 10

10 Grammar, Punctuation & Spelling: Test 1

There are **6 questions** in this test.
Give yourself **10 minutes** to answer them all.
You **may not** use a dictionary for this test.

1 We need to attend Jimmys sales meeting at 1 o'clock tomorrow

Rewrite the text above, adding in the two missing punctuation marks.

....

.... (1)

2 The sentence below has been split apart and mixed up.
It also contains one spelling mistake.

has run out of paper,	reload the paper tray for me please.
The printer	so I woud like you to

Write the sentence out, correcting the spelling mistake and putting all of the parts in the correct order.

....

.... (2)

3 Underline the joining word in the sentence below.

'Rhadika wants to go home early because she is tired.' (1)

4 Add a prefix to each word below to give it the opposite meaning.

(a) appealing .... **(b)** loyal .... (2)

5 Which of the sentences below uses commas correctly?
Put a **cross** ☒ in the correct box.

If you make a mistake, put a line through the box ☒ and mark your new answer with a cross ☒.

☐ **A** They need books computers, and tables.

☐ **B** He is cheery, generous, and always, helpful.

☐ **C** This weekend I've been to, Leeds, Newcastle and Sunderland.

☐ **D** I saw Sean, Michael and Isabel when I went out. (1)

6 The passage below contains **three** mistakes.
There is one **grammar** error, one **punctuation** error and one **spelling** error.

> My friend Joanna is worried that thiefs might target her house while she is on holiday. however, we is going to keep an eye on her house for her.

Rewrite the passage using the correct grammar, punctuation and spelling.

....

....

....

.... (3)

END OF TEST **/ 10**

Grammar, Punctuation & Spelling: Test 2

There are **6 questions** in this test.
Give yourself **10 minutes** to answer them all.
You **may not** use a dictionary for this test.

1 We will have fun when are families come to visit us.

Rewrite the sentence above, correcting any spelling mistakes.

....

.... (1)

---

2 Turn each pair of words into a single word by using an apostrophe.

(a) we are .... (1)

(b) they will .... (1)

---

3 I went to watch Ola sing in the choir She was incredible

Rewrite this sentence, adding **one** full stop and **one** exclamation mark.

....

.... (2)

4 To lose wieght, I'm going to eat less fast food and exercise more often.

Rewrite the sentence above with the spelling mistake corrected.

....

.... (1)

5 Use an appropriate joining phrase to complete the sentence below.

Abbie hates cleaning the house, ... Luke seems to love it. (1)

6 The passage below contains **three** mistakes.
There is one **grammar** error, one **punctuation** error and one **spelling** error.

> Are you having trouble with your car or van. Then you should call Spanner & Sons! One of our fully-qualified mechanics will came by as soon as possible to provide you with a profesional service.

Rewrite the passage using the correct grammar, punctuation and spelling.

....

....

....

....

.... (3)

END OF TEST **/ 10**

Structure & Format: Test 1

There is **1 question** in this test.
Give yourself **10 minutes** to answer it.
You **may not** use a dictionary for this test.

You are a writer for a food magazine.
You went to the restaurant 'Russellino's' and made the following notes:

<u>Russellino's (Italian food)</u>

Restaurant is nicely decorated
Delicious fish and fresh vegetables
Poor quality meat
Very expensive (£50!) — good value?

Write a review of Russellino's for your magazine. In your review, you should:

- describe what you enjoyed during your visit to the restaurant
- describe anything you thought the restaurant could improve on
- explain why you would or wouldn't recommend going to Russellino's.

Make a quick plan for your answer below, then write your answer on the next page.
Make sure your grammar, punctuation and spelling are correct.

Aim to write about 100 words.

END OF TEST

/ 10

Structure & Format: Test 2

There are **4 questions** in this test.
Give yourself **10 minutes** to answer them all.
You **may not** use a dictionary for this test.

1 **You have been asked to write a leaflet using the following information:**

Subject: walking in the countryside	**Format:** leaflet
Purpose: to persuade friends to walk more	**Word count:** 50 words

Circle the correct option in the sentence below.

The leaflet should be written in an impersonal / personal style. (1)

---

2 **Give two features you might expect a report to have.**

1 .... (1)

2 .... (1)

---

3 **Identify the audience and the reason for writing in each of the tasks below.**

(a) **Write an email to a pub manager asking to host an event.**

Audience ....

Purpose .... (1)

(b) **Write a leaflet advertising your band's show to people in your town.**

Audience ....

Purpose .... (1)

4 Read the email below, then answer the question.

From: Sophia.Jones@azmail.co.uk
Subject: Gift Ideas...

Hello,

I hope you've been well. I'm hoping for some advice. I have to buy my wife's birthday present and I'm struggling to decide what I should get her! I know that you two met up just last week, so did she mention wanting anything in particular? If she didn't, it's no problem, but can you tell me what you've got her? I'd hate to buy the same gift!

Cheers!

Sophia

Write a reply of around **50 words** which:

- advises Sophia on what gift to buy
- describes what gift you've already bought.

Plan your answer on a separate piece of paper, then write your answer below. Make sure your grammar, punctuation and spelling are correct.

To: Sophia.Jones@azmail.co.uk
Subject: RE: Gift Ideas...

....

....

....

....

....

....

....

....

(5)

END OF TEST

/ 10

Structure & Format: Test 3

There is **1 question** in this test.

Give yourself **10 minutes** to answer it.

You **may not** use a dictionary for this test.

You work for a local newspaper and have just been handed the poster below.

CARNIVAL COMES TO FROGHAM!

12 pm, Saturday 20th July*

- Come along and experience a festival of fun!
- All of your favourite local stores, plus a wide range of new market stalls, will be selling delicious food, drink and much, much more!
- Bring the whole family and spread some joy!

* Be sure to arrive early — parking will be limited.

Write an article about the carnival. In your article, you should:

- describe how the carnival might benefit Frogham
- describe why the carnival might be bad for Frogham
- explain if you think the carnival is good for Frogham and why.

Make a quick plan for your answer below, then write your answer on the next page. Make sure your grammar, punctuation and spelling are correct.

Aim to write about 100 words.

END OF TEST

/ 10

Structure & Format: Test 4

There is **1 question** in this test.
Give yourself **10 minutes** to answer it.
You **may not** use a dictionary for this test.

Last week, you visited 'Heart & Sole' (the main shoe store in your town) to buy your children some new school shoes.

The staff you spoke to in the shop were rude and took a long time to assist you. Additionally, the shoes you bought are already starting to fall apart.

Write a letter to complain to the manager of Heart & Sole at:
Heart & Sole, 69 Lane Road, Gantly, GW9 6JY

You should:

- describe how the staff in the shop made you feel
- explain what is wrong with the shoes that you bought
- explain to the manager what you would like them to do.

Make a quick plan for your answer below, then write your answer on the next page.
Make sure your grammar, punctuation and spelling are correct.

Aim to write about 100 words.

END OF TEST

/ 10

Structure & Format: Test 5

There are **4 questions** in this test.
Give yourself **10 minutes** to answer them all.
You **may not** use a dictionary for this test.

1 What is the purpose of a report?

....

.... (1)

2 What type of writing style would you use for each of these writing tasks?
Circle the correct option for each task.

(a) A letter to the council about council tax. **Formal / Informal** (1)

(b) A letter congratulating your friend. **Formal / Informal** (1)

(c) An email to your employer about time off. **Formal / Informal** (1)

3 Read the following passage from a parent's email to a teacher.

> Dear Mr Grintles,
> I am emailing you due to concerns over my son's progress in your class. His latest report says that he is falling behind. Would you be available one evening next week to discuss this in more depth?

Write an appropriate ending to the email above.

.... (1)

4 Read the article below, then answer the question.

> **TRAFFIC INCIDENT — MARCH 26 — SWADDLETON:**
>
> On Sunday, March 26, there was an accident on the main road outside of Swaddleton. Reports suggest that a lorry lost control as it rounded the bend and struck a barrier on the side of the road. There was little traffic at the time, so nobody was harmed. This has been the latest in a string of incidents on that stretch of road. In the last few weeks alone, there have been incidents involving trucks, cars and motorbikes. Questions are beginning to be asked about why it keeps happening, and many local figures are demanding swift action from the council to slow drivers down.

Write an email of around **50 words** to the council which:

- explains why changes need to be made
- suggests changes that could be made.

Plan your answer on a separate piece of paper, then write your answer below. Make sure your grammar, punctuation and spelling are correct.

To:

Subject:

....

....

....

....

....

....

....

(5)

END OF TEST

/ 10

Structure & Format: Test 6

There is **1 question** in this test.
Give yourself **10 minutes** to answer it.
You **may not** use a dictionary for this test.

You were in the crowd when a celebrity visited your town. The celebrity had donated a lot of money towards the renovation of the local library and had come to help reopen it. There was a huge crowd and people applauded the celebrity as they cut the ribbon.

You work for the local paper and have been asked to write a report of what you saw.

In your report, you must include:

- when and where the celebrity visited
- what the celebrity's donations were spent on
- whether the visit was successful and why.

Make a quick plan for your answer below, then write your answer on the next page.
Make sure your grammar, punctuation and spelling are correct.

Aim to write about 100 words.

....

....

....

....

....

....

....

....

....

....

....

....

....

....

....

....

....

....

END OF TEST

/ 10

Structure & Format: Test 7

There is **1 question** in this test.
Give yourself **10 minutes** to answer it.
You **may not** use a dictionary for this test.

You have been invited to perform at the event below.

BALLROOM BRILLIANCE
Entry only £5 — kids go free!

- Some of the best dancers around
- Performances to suit everyone's tastes
- Food and drink served all night

Don't forget to buy your tickets — it's fun for all the family!

After performing, you decide to write about the experience for your blog.
In your blog post, you should:

- describe the event
- explain how your performance went
- give your opinion on whether the event was a success and why.

Make a quick plan for your answer below, then write your answer on the next page.
Make sure your grammar, punctuation and spelling are correct.

Aim to write about 100 words.

END OF TEST

/ 10

Structure & Format: Test 8

There is **1 question** in this test.
Give yourself **10 minutes** to answer it.
You **may not** use a dictionary for this test.

You want to apply for the job below.

Retail shop assistant wanted

You will be working on the shop floor, advising customers and selling products.

Qualities we are looking for:

- Friendliness — you need to be comfortable communicating with customers.
- Organisation — you'll need to monitor stock and keep the shop floor tidy.

Let us know about any relevant experience you have.

To apply, write to: Emperor Clothes, Main Street, London, SX3 6UJ.

Write a letter to the manager of Emperor Clothes in which you apply for the job.
Remember to:

- describe your experience, qualifications and skills
- explain why you are suitable for the job.

Make a quick plan for your answer below, then write your answer on the next page.
Make sure your grammar, punctuation and spelling are correct.

Aim to write about 100 words.

END OF TEST

/ 10

Structure & Format: Test 9

There are **3 questions** in this test.
Give yourself **10 minutes** to answer them all.
You **may not** use a dictionary for this test.

1 Circle the correct option in the sentences below.

(a) You **should / shouldn't** start a new paragraph when the topic changes. (1)

(b) A new paragraph always begins on **a different / the same** line. (1)

---

2 Read the passage below, then answer the questions.

> Hey James,
>
> I hope that you're doing okay. Do you still fancy buying the spare equipment that I've had lying about in the garage for ages?
>
> See you soon!
> Shoaib

(a) What type of text is the passage above?

.... (1)

(b) Rewrite each of the phrases below using more formal language.

'Do you still fancy buying'

.... (1)

'See you soon!'

.... (1)

3 You have just received the email below.

> Hello again,
>
> As we previously discussed on the phone, Pinton Council have just opened a new community vegetable garden with 100 plots. We would like you to produce a leaflet advertising the garden to the local community. Plots can be shared by multiple owners and can be hired through the council's website.
>
> Yours faithfully,
> Margaret Gobbins — Pinton Council

Write a leaflet of around **50 words** which:

- encourages people to rent a plot in the community vegetable garden
- suggests what people could grow in their plot.

Plan your answer on a separate piece of paper, then write your answer below.
Make sure your grammar, punctuation and spelling are correct.

....

....

....

....

....

....

....

.... (5)

END OF TEST **/ 10**

Answers

Part 1 — Reading

Section One — How Texts Present Ideas

Test 1 — Pages 2-3

1 You should have crossed: C
To instruct people how to plant trees
(1 mark)

2 Touch the roots
(1 mark)
Try to lift the tree up by its leaves
(1 mark)

3 A numbered list
(1 mark)

4 Over 100 people
(1 mark)

5 Opinion
(1 mark)

6 You should have crossed: A, D
Rhetorical question
Command
(1 mark for one correct, 2 marks for two correct)

Test 2 — Pages 4-5

1 Paragraphs
(1 mark)

2 You should have crossed: C, D
Rule of three
Exclamation
(1 mark for one correct, 2 marks for two correct)

3 You should have crossed: B, C
The Hydra 2E has over 1000 reviews.
'I bought myself a Hydra 2E'
(1 mark for one correct, 2 marks for two correct)

4 a) You could write any one of these:
- Both reviews say that the phone is too big.
- Both reviews say the phone cannot fit in your pocket.
- Both reviews say that the phone is cheap.

(1 mark)

b) Answers may vary, for example:
Review 1:
- 'This phone is cheap'
- 'admittedly, it doesn't fit in my pocket'
- 'difficult to carry around without a bag'

(1 mark)
Review 2:
- 'it was cheap'
- 'I can't fit it in my pocket'
- 'it is too big to hold in my hand'

(1 mark)

Test 3 — Pages 6-7

1 Answers may vary, for example: 'Volunteers serve food to people who need it' or 'Volunteers work in a team'.
(1 mark)

2 a) Impersonal
(1 mark)
b) Personal
(1 mark)

3 a) 'What can you do to support us?'
(1 mark)
b) 'What is a food bank?'
(1 mark)

4 You should have crossed: A, B
It's easy to donate food to the food bank.
It's better to donate food than volunteer.
(1 mark for one correct, 2 marks for two correct)

5 You should have crossed: C
To persuade people to donate or volunteer
(1 mark)

Test 4 — Pages 8-9

1 You should have crossed: B
Alliteration
(1 mark)

2 Writing recipes for a student magazine.
(1 mark)

3 Descriptive
(1 mark)
You could write any one of these:
- 'excellent cups of tea'
- 'it truly feels like a second home'
- 'the welcoming smell of coffee and freshly-baked biscuits'
- 'The walls are lined with bookcases'
- 'signs that advertise "Gorgeously Gooey Brownies"'

(1 mark)

4 You should have crossed: B, C
'What's changing?'
'everyone can still get out and about'
(1 mark for one correct, 2 marks for two correct)

5 'Educate, Innovate, Excel'
(1 mark)

6 It suffered flood damage.
(1 mark)

Test 5 — Pages 10-11

1 You could write any two of these:
- Headings
- Subheadings
- Bullet points

(1 mark for one correct, 2 marks for two correct)

2 You could write any of these:
- 'Work experience can be really useful'
- 'only if you choose the right company'

- 'I found some of my work experience fairly poor'
- 'I want to be a receptionist'
- 'I didn't learn many skills that are useful for the job'
- It 'was really useful'

(1 mark)

3 You should have crossed: D
'Show enthusiasm.'
(1 mark)

4 You could write any of these:
- Both articles say that work experience can be useful.
- Both articles say that work experience allows you to confirm whether you are interested in the job.
- Both articles recommend asking questions.

(1 mark)

5 a) Answers may vary, for example:
- Whether work experience is essential.
- Whether work experience gives you useful skills.

(1 mark)

b) Answers may vary, for example:
Article A:
'getting some work experience is vital'
'Work experience also lets you develop skills which are useful for the role'
(1 mark)
Article B:
'Work experience can be really useful, but only if you choose the right company.'
'I didn't learn many skills that are useful for the job.'
(1 mark)

Test 6 — Pages 12-13

1 'Matches take place on Saturday or Sunday afternoons.'
(1 mark)

2 a) Menu / Tab
(Accept 'Contact Us!' button)
(1 mark)
b) Search bar
(1 mark)

3 You should have crossed: A, C
North Sea Hockey Club has four teams in total.
There is a social event every month.
(1 mark for one correct, 2 marks for two correct)

4 You should have crossed: B
Direct address
(1 mark)

5 a) Ulverbury
(1 mark)
b) A table
(Accept 'text box')
(1 mark)

Test 7 — Pages 14-15

1 You could write any one of these positives:
- Inventing new ideas for parties
- Seeing customers enjoy the parties

(1 mark)
You could write any one of these negatives:
- It is stressful.
- Working to specific dates can be challenging.

(1 mark)

2 You should have crossed: A
'Well, it's not all laughter and cake'
(1 mark)

3 The local youth group
(1 mark)

4 Any suitable replacement. For example:
- looked after
- watched

(1 mark)

5 You could write any one of these:
- a soft drink
- a piece of homemade cake

(1 mark)

6 a) Children under four
(1 mark)
b) A footnote
(1 mark)

Test 8 — Pages 16-17

1 The northwest
(1 mark)

2 Lake Windermere
(1 mark)

3 Train
(1 mark)

4 You could write any two of these:
- A heading
- Subheadings / Numbered List
- Paragraphs

(1 mark for one correct, 2 marks for two correct)

5 You should have crossed: D
To instruct the reader on how to get to the Lake District
(1 mark)

6 You should have crossed: A, B
It is permitted to kayak in the Lake District.
Kayaking can be a group activity.
(1 mark for one correct, 2 marks for two correct)

Section Two — Reading for Detail

Test 1 — Pages 18-19

1 a) 'Step back in time...'
(1 mark)
b) 'Get outdoors...'
(1 mark)

2 You could write any two of these:
- medieval churches
- French cafés
- Mareau Chateau OR a sixteenth-century castle

(1 mark for one correct, 2 marks for two correct)

3 £28
(1 mark)

4 Answers may vary, for example:
- picturesque
- blissful

(1 mark)

5 You should have crossed: A
To show that the words are speech
(1 mark)

6 Lake Antaux
(1 mark)

Test 2 — Pages 20-21

1 A few weeks
(1 mark)

2 To show that the sentence is a question
(1 mark)

3 a) Any suitable replacement. For example:
- refused
- turned down

(1 mark)

b) Any suitable replacement. For example:
- work
- join forces

(1 mark)

4 Answers may vary, for example:
'it's really de-motivating'
'I always feel left in the dark'
'I want to concede defeat'
(1 mark)

5 a) E.g. Matthew thinks the best method for getting a job is applying for lots of jobs, but Nadiya thinks you should just apply for jobs you have a genuine interest in.
(1 mark)

b) Answers may vary, for example:
Matthew's email:
- 'I've been applying for various jobs for a few weeks now'
- 'I think it's best to send out lots of job applications'

Nadiya's email:
- 'don't just apply for loads of jobs'
- 'Apply for jobs you have a genuine interest in'

(1 mark for one correct, 2 marks for two correct)

Test 3 — Pages 22-23

1 Answers may vary, for example:
- disease
- disorder

(1 mark)

2 a) Becca
(1 mark)

b) Abdul
(1 mark)

3 You should have crossed: A, C
To show the end of the sentence
To show a strong emotion
(1 mark)

4 a) Both agree that gluten-free food is expensive.
(1 mark)

b) Becca's post:
'they're also more expensive'
Abdul's post:
'it's crazy that a loaf of gluten-free bread costs £3!'
(1 mark for one correct, 2 marks for two correct)

Test 4 — Pages 24-25

1 'Fun Fusion' classes only involve one form of exercise. — False
'Fun Fusion' classes take place on Tuesdays. — True
(1 mark for one correct, 2 marks for two correct)

2 Answers may vary, for example:
- It suggests 'Fun Fusion' makes people feel happy.
- It suggests that the exercise is done in groups.
- It suggests that members of the class follow a leader's instructions / copy a leader's demonstrations.

(1 mark)

3 a) Delton Sports Centre
(1 mark)

b) Subheading
(1 mark)

4 Answers may vary, for example:
- suited to
- made for

(1 mark)

5 a) You should have crossed: B
To persuade people to sign up to 'Fun Fusion'
(1 mark)

b) You could write any one of these:
- 'HAVE FUN, GET FIT!'
- 'Do you want to get into shape without spending hours in the gym?'
- 'Do you want to enjoy exercise rather than slogging away on a treadmill?'
  - 'We have a solution: sign up to Fun Fusion classes today!'
- 'Break out of the boredom of your exercise routine with Fun Fusion'
- 'you work twice as hard, and with twice the fun!'
- 'Come along on Tuesday'
- 'try out Fun Fusion for just £4'

(1 mark)

Part 2 — Writing

Section One — Grammar

Test 1 — Pages 26-27

1 a) a
(1 mark)

b) an
(1 mark)

2 a) 'is'
(1 mark)

b) There <u>are</u> three people doing the interview.
(1 mark)

3 The bus should <u>have</u> been here 10 minutes ago.
(1 mark)

4 The recipe seems perfect for me because it looks delicious. However, it is a bit too expensive for my budget.
(1 mark for one sentence correct, 2 marks for both sentences correct)

5 I completed my paperwork last week.
(1 mark)

6 • although
• after
• until
(1 mark for one correct, 2 marks for all correct)

Test 2 — Pages 28-29

1 • so
• nor
• but
(1 mark for one correct, 2 marks for all correct)

2 a) Pavel tried to pay his rent.
(1 mark)
b) They needed to find a new job.
(1 mark)
c) Emily ran every morning before work.
(Also accept 'Emily went running every morning before work.')
(1 mark)

3 wins
(1 mark)

4 I went to pick up my dry cleaning, then I took my children to school and finally I cleaned the kitchen.
(1 mark for two parts in the correct order, 2 marks for all parts in the correct order)

5 a) I will have seen that film.
(Also accept 'I will see that film.')
(1 mark)
b) Shania will not be very impressed.
(1 mark)

Test 3 — Pages 30-31

1 a) barks
(1 mark)
b) want
(1 mark)

2 a) Verb: sprayed
Person: Megan
(1 mark)
b) Verb: operated
Person: her patient
(1 mark)

3 It is getting very cold in the evenings.
(1 mark)

4 Any appropriate verb, for example:
• finished
• updated
(1 mark)

5 You should have crossed: C
I will go to the meeting that has been arranged.
(1 mark)

6 I am visiting my cousin to see their new house.
(1 mark)

7 a) The verbs are in different tenses / are not consistent with each other.
(1 mark)
b) Munira fell off her bike, but she only scraped her knee.
(1 mark)

Section Two — Punctuation

Test 1 — Pages 32-33

1 You should have crossed: C
She was scared because she had never driven at night.
(1 mark)

2 I need to pack a suit, a shirt, a toothbrush and a hairbrush.
(1 mark for both correct)

3 a) It's
(1 mark)
b) its
(1 mark)

4 a) There should be an apostrophe in 'youre' to show where a letter has been removed.
(1 mark)
b) "Oh, that is so generous of you. You're very kind."
(1 mark)

5 Answers may vary, for example:
Are you going out for a meal tonight?
(1 mark)

6 a) There were a lot of cars on the main road to Manchester.
(1 mark for both correct)
b) Antonio needs to send a parcel to his mother in Italy.
(1 mark for both correct)
c) During her break on Monday, Jane went for a short walk.
(1 mark for all correct)

Test 2 — pages 34-35

1 a) I prefer quiet villages to London's busy streets.
(1 mark)
b) All three of Kevin's dogs are labradors.
(1 mark)

2 I thought the show would be a bit more expensive. Are the children's tickets really that cheap? That's absolutely amazing value!
(1 mark for each correct punctuation mark)

3 Please show me how I should fill out this form.
(1 mark for both correct)

4 As Obafemi rushed around the shop, he looked at the list of things that Mary had asked him to buy. He started to panic — the shop was going to close soon. Could he find all of the items in time?
(1 mark for each correct punctuation mark)

5 a) There should be a comma to separate the items in the list.
(1 mark)

b) The apartment has a bedroom, a kitchen and a bathroom.
(1 mark)

Section Three — Spelling

Test 1 — Pages 36-37

1 Some people didn't get their packages.
(1 mark)

2 a) achieve
(1 mark)
b) ceiling
(1 mark)
c) science
(1 mark)

3 a) describe
(1 mark)
b) surprise
(1 mark)

4 You should have crossed: B commanding
(1 mark)

5 Rosie was disappointed when her show was cancelled. Her friends saw this and tried to cheer her up. After spending the rest of the day laughing and joking with them, Rosie began to feel better.
(1 mark for each spelling mistake corrected, 3 marks in total)

Test 2 — pages 38-39

1 introduction
(1 mark)

2 He was tired and stressed, which made him unnecessarily rude.
(1 mark)

3 a) deer
(1 mark)
b) children
(1 mark)
c) lorries
(1 mark)

4 You shouldn't try to do too many jobs at the same time.
(1 mark)

5 stunning
(1 mark)

6 Declan had just accepted an offer for his antique knives and felt pleased. He knew that the sale would be good for his business.
(1 mark for each spelling mistake corrected, 3 marks in total)

Section Four — Grammar, Punctuation & Spelling

Test 1 — Pages 40-41

1 We need to attend Jimmy's sales meeting at 1 o'clock tomorrow.
(1 mark)

2 The printer has run out of paper, so would like you to reload the paper tray for me please.
(1 mark for putting the parts in the correct order, 1 mark for correcting the spelling mistake)

3 Rhadika wants to go home early because she is tired.
(1 mark)

4 a) unappealing
b) disloyal
(1 mark for each correct spelling, 2 marks in total)

5 You should have crossed: D
I saw Sean, Michael and Isabel when I went out.
(1 mark)

6 My friend Joanna is worried that thieves might target her house while she is on holiday. However, we are going to keep an eye on her house for her.
(1 mark for each correction, 3 marks in total)

Test 2 — Pages 42-43

1 We will have fun when our families come to visit us.
(1 mark)

2 a) we're
(1 mark)
b) they'll
(1 mark)

3 I went to watch Ola sing in the choir. She was incredible!
(1 mark for each correct punctuation mark)

4 To lose weight, I'm going to eat less fast food and exercise more often.
(1 mark)

5 Abbie hates cleaning the house, but Luke seems to love it.
(Also accept 'and' or 'yet')
(1 mark)

6 Are you having trouble with your car or van? Then you should call Spanner & Sons! One of our fully-qualified mechanics will come by as soon as possible to provide you with a professional service.
(1 mark for each correction, 3 marks in total)

Section Five — Structure & Format

Test 1 — Pages 44-45

Review Writing Task

There are up to 6 marks available for the structure and content of your review. A top-level answer will:

- Communicate information clearly in a polite, formal style.
- Be written in full sentences, and use a range of sentence types.
- Have a clear and logical structure, using paragraphs when appropriate.
- Include a title to show what the review is about, e.g. 'Russellino's: Looks Better Than It Tastes'.
- Describe what you enjoyed about the restaurant, e.g. 'The dining room is decorated tastefully and is very pleasing to look at.'

- Describe what you thought the restaurant could improve on, e.g. 'My steak was very fatty and was not cooked to my liking.'
- Explain why you would or wouldn't recommend going to Russellino's, e.g. 'I would not recommend going to Russellino's because the standard of the meat dishes does not live up to the expensive price.'
- You could include your name to show who wrote the review.

(6 marks)

There are up to 4 marks available for the spelling, punctuation and grammar of your answer.
A top-level answer will:
- Use grammar and punctuation correctly and with few errors.
- Spell words, including specialist words, correctly and with few errors.

(4 marks)

Test 2 — Pages 46-47

1 personal
(1 mark)

2 Any two of:
- Formal language
- Facts and information
- Headings
- Subheadings
- Bullet points / Numbered lists

(2 marks)

3 a) Audience — a pub manager
Purpose — to ask to host an event
(1 mark)
b) Audience — people in your town
Purpose — to advertise your band's show
(1 mark)

4 Email Writing Task
There are up to 3 marks available for the structure and content of your email.
A top-level answer will:
- Communicate information clearly in a friendly, informal style.
- Be written in full sentences, and have a clear and logical structure (using paragraphs if appropriate).
- Start with an informal greeting, e.g. 'Hi Sophia'.
- Give advice on what Sophia should buy for her wife, e.g. 'Your wife mentioned that she needs a new coat, so you could buy her a nice coat for her birthday.'
- Describe the gift you have bought, e.g. 'I've bought her some earrings that I thought would suit her.'
- End with an informal and friendly sign-off, e.g. 'See you soon,' and your name.

(3 marks)

There are up to 2 marks available for the spelling, punctuation and grammar of your answer.
A top-level answer will:
- Use grammar and punctuation correctly and with few errors.
- Spell words, including specialist words, correctly and with few errors.

(2 marks)

Test 3 — Pages 48-49

Article Writing Task

There are up to 6 marks available for the structure and content of your article. A top-level answer will:
- Communicate information clearly in a polite style.
- Be written in full sentences, and use a range of sentence types.
- Have a clear and logical structure, using paragraphs when appropriate.
- Have a suitable heading, e.g. 'Does Frogham Need a Carnival?'
- Use subheadings to separate different sections.
- Lay out information clearly, e.g. use numbered lists and put quotation marks around quotes.
- Describe how the carnival might benefit Frogham, e.g. 'The carnival could bring increased business for Frogham's local stores, providing a boost for local businesses.'
- Describe potential downsides of the carnival, e.g. 'The number of people visiting the carnival might limit parking for Frogham residents who are not attending the carnival.'
- Explain whether you think the carnival will be good or bad for Frogham, e.g. 'The carnival will be good for Frogham because it will bring in extra business, as well as providing local families with an enjoyable day out.'

(6 marks)

There are up to 4 marks available for the spelling, punctuation and grammar of your answer.
A top-level answer will:
- Use grammar and punctuation correctly and with few errors.
- Spell words, including specialist words, correctly and with few errors.

(4 marks)

Test 4 — Pages 50-51

Letter Writing Task

There are up to 6 marks available for the structure and content of your letter. A top-level answer will:
- Communicate information clearly in a polite, formal style.
- Be written in full sentences, and use a range of sentence types.
- Have a clear and logical structure, using paragraphs if appropriate.
- Give your name, address and the date at the top right-hand side of the page.

- Give the store's full address on the left-hand side of the page, underneath your information:
  The Manager
  Heart & Sole
  69 Lane Road
  Gantly
  GW9 6JY
- Start with a formal greeting, e.g. 'Dear Sir / Madam'.
- Describe how the shop staff made you feel, e.g. 'The staff ignored my requests for help for a long time, which made me feel like I was not a valued customer in your store.'
- Explain what was wrong with the shoes that you bought, e.g. 'The shoes that I bought are not of a high quality. I have only had them for one week and the soles are already worn and full of holes.'
- Explain what you want the manager to do, e.g. 'Due to my poor experience, I would like a full refund for the shoes that I purchased.'
- End with 'Yours faithfully' and your full name.

  (6 marks)

There are up to 4 marks available for the spelling, punctuation and grammar of your answer.
A top-level answer will:
- Use grammar and punctuation correctly and with few errors.
- Spell words, including specialist words, correctly and with few errors.

  (4 marks)

Test 5 — Pages 52-53

1 To give information or facts to the reader.
  (1 mark)

2 a) Formal
  (1 mark)
  b) Informal
  (1 mark)
  c) Formal
  (1 mark)

3 'Yours sincerely' and your full name.
  (1 mark)

4 Email Writing Task:

There are up to 3 marks available for the structure and content of your email.
A top-level answer will:
- Communicate information clearly in a polite, formal style.
- Be written in full sentences, and have a clear and logical structure (using paragraphs if appropriate).
- Have an email address or name in the 'To' box, e.g. 'Swaddleton Council'.
- Have an appropriate 'Subject', e.g. 'Traffic Incidents'.
- Start with a formal greeting, e.g. 'Dear Sir / Madam'.
- Explain why changes need to be made, e.g. 'Changes need to be made because there have been too many accidents on that stretch of road in recent times.'
- Suggest the changes that could be made, e.g. 'The council should install speed cameras to discourage careless drivers from driving too fast.'
- End with 'Yours faithfully' and your full name.

  (3 marks)

There are up to 2 marks available for the spelling, punctuation and grammar of your answer. A top-level answer will:
- Use grammar and punctuation correctly and with few errors.
- Spell words, including specialist words, correctly and with few errors.

  (2 marks)

Test 6 — Pages 54-55
Report Writing Task

There are up to 6 marks available for the structure and content of your report. A top-level answer will:
- Communicate information clearly in a polite style.
- Be written in full sentences, and use a range of sentence types.
- Have a clear and logical structure, using paragraphs when appropriate.
- Have a title to show what the report is about, e.g. 'Famous Face Adds Sparkle to Grand Reopening'.
- Use subheadings to separate different sections of your report.
- Explain when and where the celebrity visited, e.g. 'The visit took place two days ago, and the celebrity popped into several local shops on their way to the newly-renovated library.'
- Explain what the celebrity's donated money was spent on, e.g. 'The money was spent on expanding the library's range of books, as well as a new reading room for younger children.'
- Explain whether you think the visit was successful and why, e.g. 'The visit was an overwhelming success because the town now has a library that is fit for purpose and the celebrity was well-liked by the local people.'

  (6 marks)

There are up to 4 marks available for the spelling, punctuation and grammar of your answer.
A top-level answer will:
- Use grammar and punctuation correctly and with few errors.
- Spell words, including specialist words, correctly and with few errors.

  (4 marks)

Test 7 — Pages 56-57
Blog Post Writing Task

There are up to 6 marks available for the structure and content of your blog post. A top-level answer will:
- Communicate information clearly.
- Be written in full sentences, and use a range of sentence types.
- Have a clear and logical structure, using paragraphs if appropriate.
- Have a title to show what your blog post is about, e.g. 'Ballroom Brilliance: My Experience'
- Perhaps start with an informal greeting, e.g. 'Hi guys'.
- You could use subheadings to separate different sections of your blog post.
- A description of the event, e.g. 'The evening featured a range of dances that were performed to excellent music. You could watch anything: waltzes, salsas, tangos and foxtrots were on display, as well as some modern dance.'
- Explain how you think your performance went, e.g. 'My own performance went brilliantly! All of my hard work and practice really paid off and I had a lot of fun.'
- Give your opinion on whether the event as a whole was a success, e.g. 'The whole night was a great success because everyone looked like they were having a great time. People of all ages had seen some new dances by the end of the night!'

(6 marks)

There are up to 4 marks available for the spelling, punctuation and grammar of your answer.
A top-level answer will:
- Use grammar and punctuation correctly and with few errors.
- Spell words, including specialist words, correctly and with few errors.

(4 marks)

Test 8 — Pages 58-59
Letter Writing Task

There are up to 6 marks available for the structure and content of your letter. A top-level answer will:
- Communicate information clearly in a polite, formal style.
- Be written in full sentences, and use a range of sentence types.
- Have a clear and logical structure, using paragraphs if appropriate.
- Give your name, address and the date at the top right-hand side of the page.
- Give the shop's full address on the left-hand side of the page, underneath your information:
  The Manager
  Emperor Clothes
  Main Street
  London
  SX3 6UJ
- Start with a formal greeting, e.g. 'Dear Sir / Madam'.
- Describe your experience, qualifications and skills, e.g. 'I have worked in retail for two years. and have won an award for my customer service skills.'
- Explain why you are suitable for the job, e.g. 'I am very friendly and love helping customers with any issues that they have.'
- End with 'Yours faithfully' and your full name.

(6 marks)

There are up to 4 marks available for the spelling, punctuation and grammar of your answer.
A top-level answer will:
- Use grammar and punctuation correctly and with few errors.
- Spell words, including specialist words, correctly and with few errors.

(4 marks)

Test 9 — Pages 60-61

1 should
(1 mark)
a different
(1 mark)

2 a) Letter / Email
(1 mark)
b) Answers may vary, e.g.
- Do you still wish to purchase
- Yours sincerely,

(1 mark)

3 Leaflet Writing Task:

There are up to 3 marks available for the structure and content of your leaflet.
A top-level answer will:
- Be written in full sentences, and have a clear and logical structure (using paragraphs if appropriate).
- Have a title to show what the leaflet is about, e.g. 'Grab Your Own Plot TODAY'.
- Use subheadings to separate different sections of the leaflet.
- Present key information clearly, e.g. by using statistics, bullet points or numbered lists.
- Encourage people to rent a plot in the garden, e.g. 'Why not become more eco-friendly and grow your own food on a personal plot of land?'
- Suggest what people could grow in their plot, e.g. 'You could grow anything from parsnips to pumpkins, or carrots to coriander.'

(3 marks)

There are up to 2 marks available for the spelling, punctuation and grammar of your answer. A top-level answer will:
- Use grammar and punctuation correctly and with few errors.
- Spell words, including specialist words, correctly and with few errors.

(2 marks)

Progress Chart

When you've completed and marked a test, put your score in the correct place.

Part 1 — Reading

How Texts Present Ideas	
Test 1	/ 8
Test 2	/ 8
Test 3	/ 8
Test 4	/ 8
Test 5	/ 8
Test 6	/ 8
Test 7	/ 8
Test 8	/ 8

Reading for Detail	
Test 1	/ 8
Test 2	/ 8
Test 3	/ 8
Test 4	/ 8

Part 2 — Writing

Grammar	
Test 1	/ 10
Test 2	/ 10
Test 3	/ 10

Punctuation	
Test 1	/ 10
Test 2	/ 10

Spelling	
Test 1	/ 10
Test 2	/ 10

Grammar, Punctuation & Spelling	
Test 1	/ 10
Test 2	/ 10

Structure & Format	
Test 1	/ 10
Test 2	/ 10
Test 3	/ 10
Test 4	/ 10
Test 5	/ 10
Test 6	/ 10
Test 7	/ 10
Test 8	/ 10
Test 9	/ 10

Once you've filled in your score, use the table below for some advice on what to try next.

Mark		
Reading	Writing	
0-3	0-4	You're not quite there yet, but keep going. Make sure you understand where you went wrong before you try another test.
4-6	5-8	Almost there — revisit the topics you got wrong, then try another test to see if you can score even higher next time.
7-8	9-10	Well done, this is a great score! Give yourself a pat on the back, then have a go at another test — practice makes perfect!